A Guided Pra

Grounding

Coming Home to Your Self

Nell Arnaud

Copyright © 2010 by Nell Arnaud
All rights reserved.

Table of Contents

Table of Contents 3
Foreword 7
Thanks and Acknowledgement 11

Chapter 1 – What is Grounding

What is Grounding 15
A Simple Grounding Meditation 19
Grounding and Self Healing Meditation 23

Chapter 2 – Keeping it Simple

Keeping it Simple 29
The Journey Begins 30
Grounding in the Classroom 32

Chapter 3 – The Benefits of Grounding

The Benefits of Grounding 35
Grounding and Tennis 44

Chapter 4 – Helpful Hints

Helpful Hints..47

Dr. Liu's Chi Gong Exercise for Stress...49

Grounding Meditation with Dr. Liu's Chi Gong Exercise for Stress..53

Suggestions when Grounding is Difficult..55

Situations when you really need Grounding.......................................57

Suggestions when Grounding is Impossible.......................................58

Chapter 5 – Refining Grounding

Refining Grounding 63

Visuals for your Grounding Cord...64

Visualizing Earth Energy..66

Grounding Sensations 67

Symptoms of Blocks and Discordant Energies in the Body................68

Grounding Affirmations 71

Chapter 6 – The Golden Flame Meditation

The Golden Flame...73

The Golden Flame Cleansing Meditation..74

Healing the Grounding Cord..77

The Golden Flame Meditation for Healing the Grounding Cord........78

Other Uses for the Golden Flame...80

Chapter 7 – Grounding and Healing

Grounding and Healing 83

Grounding with Ruby 85

Ruby Grounding and Dealing with People with an Attitude..............86

Ruby Grounding Meditation 88

Other Elements for Grounding and Healing....................................90

Chapter 8 – Grounding and Self-Responsibility

Grounding and Self-Responsibility 93

Stop the War inside Yourself 95

Grounding into Liquid Silver Forgiveness 98

Liquid Silver Forgiveness Healing Meditation 100

Chapter 9 – Grounding and Creation

Grounding and Creation..103

Grounding and Creation Meditation 104

Grounding and the California Redwoods 106

Grounding and Creation in Mt. Shasta...109

Chapter 10 – F A Q s

Frequently Asked Questions..112-128

Grounding . . . Coming Home To Your *Self*

Foreword

I began the process of Grounding in the early '80s while living in San Francisco. It was there I began my studies as a clairvoyant and energy healer. That was almost 30 years ago. At the start of this incredible journey into the world of perceiving and interpreting the rich symbols and colors of the subtle realms, the very first process I was taught was a Grounding technique. In order for a clairvoyant to feel safe and secure as one ventures into these altered states of perception, Grounding was taught and frequently reinforced for its importance to reassure, nurture and stabilize the physical, emotional bodies and all aspects of the self to be comfortable with the process of seeing

Grounding facilitates clear perception and insight in every aspect of one's life. The more I worked with it in

Grounding ... Coming Home To Your *Self*

my personal life, the more I realized that Grounding was not just for clairvoyants. This fundamental process worked really well in my relationships with others, in communication, in actualizing my goals, in my nursing career, and in my work as an elementary school teacher. Literally, everything in my life worked better from a Grounded place.

Nursing and teaching children are two of the most stressful occupations one can have. Yet, I reflect on all those years of unbelievably demanding work and how I consciously tried to integrate being Grounded as I interacted with either educating children or managing the myriads of issues for people with major health challenges. I thought if I could be fully present, Grounded and integrated within myself in these situations, I could do it anywhere.

I share with you my journey and many experiences that positively changed my life. My daily routine flowed so much better if I started the day with a simple Grounding technique. Even one to five minutes of Grounding in the morning seemed to alter the course of the entire day to make everything feel right. In

Foreword

addition, if I consciously Grounded from time to time throughout the day, I noticed more synchronicity, better communication and I more fully enjoyed participating in the flow of my life.

Since I found it to be so helpful, I began teaching classes and guiding people how to Ground. It seemed this information was too valuable and everyone should be aware of this. After all, Grounding is a fundamental connection that we all should have. Over the years, I saw this process empower the lives of my clients and students in so many ways.

As you gain a better understanding and awareness of Grounding, you'll learn to transform even hardship into energies that are supportive and help you to grow and be committed to living your life in a more dedicated way. Use this book as a guide for supporting your efforts to discover your fundamental connection to the energies of the Earth as a basis for your life. You'll also learn how to do much of your personal healing work through your Grounding connection. If more people work on their personal issues, it takes these kinds of issues from the planet as a whole. Time for us all to get to work and get Grounded!

Grounding . . . Coming Home To Your *Self*

Grounding is a process whereby you learn to take better care of yourself and be responsible for your life—which feels very much like coming home to your Self. This is not a quick fix, but rather a commitment to the quality of your personal life and well-being, which is very much worth striving for. Over time you will see results. You are building a better relationship to your Self, the health of your body, mind and emotions, your personal life and how you interact with others. Grounding brings increased awareness to your environment, to the forces of nature, to the Earth and its creatures. By being more present, you enhance your personal life and change the world to a place where you participate more fully in a more committed way. You just need to make the decision and commit to the goal...

Nell Arnaud
Mt. Shasta, CA
May 2010

Thanks and Acknowledgement

There have been many teachers in my life for whom I'm grateful of their influence on my ability to live in my body from a Grounded place—I'd like to acknowledge and thank Francesca and Michael McCartney of the Academy of Intuitive Studies for being excellent teachers and initially introducing me to these basic concepts. Thanks to Carol May of Lotus Grid for her immense influence in my life as a healer, to Dr. Johannes Liu for being such a master healer and teacher and to Fred Payne for being an incredible healer, teacher, friend and support system. These 5 are some of the most remarkable master healers and teachers I've had the privilege of learning from and working with. Thanks to the Artists Conference Network and all my delightful women and men friends who have very beautifully supported my creative process. Much gratitude to Liz Atteberry for extending her vast

Grounding ... Coming Home To Your *Self*

talents, abilities, editing skills and professional expertise in design and book publishing to this project. My thanks and acknowledgment to Kippy Spilker, of Geminai Graphics and Photography for her creativity and expertise in the book cover, editions and lay-out. I want to thank my friends Judy Ogden, Nita Mcauley, Dennis Patterson, and my sister Betty Roy for all their help with editing. I acknowledge and thank Michael Aiello for her help with demonstrating the Chi Gong poses and for being such a good friend and support. Thanks to Judy Montgomery for her friendship and her assistance over the years. I've had the privilege of working with determined light-seekers as clients and students over the years, whom I've shared intimate moments. Thank you for opening your life to me. I've learned so much from private sessions and teaching classes over the years. Our interactions have been some of my finest inspirations for furthering this work.

My greatest teacher of all time has been the power and force of Creation that permeates all things. My most profound teachers were Mt. Tamalpais, Tennessee Valley in Mill Valley, CA, the Marin Headlands, the red rocks of Sedona and the hiking trails leading me to

Thanks and Acknowledgement

the breath-taking meadows and waterfalls of Mt. Shasta. I've been a hiker of some very awe inspiring places on Earth, and it was in the many miles of nature trails that I learned to feel a connection to everything and from there to establish a more profound relationship to the Earth and ultimately to myself. This has been and continues to be my healing, my companion, my spiritual path, my nourishment, my inspiration...

Grounding . . . Coming Home To Your *Self*

Chapter 1
What is Grounding?

Grounding is a state of being integrated—body, mind and spirit while aligning with the energies of the Earth. This is a basic fundamental connection that everyone should have, so it's very important to establish this alignment. Do you know how it feels to be truly Grounded? Are you aware of the extensive list of benefits that Grounding provides? In this book, you'll examine why you'd want to live your life from this state at all times. You'll be taught how to do much of your personal healing through your Grounding connection. You'll also be shown how to make the world a better place through your consciousness about being Grounded. Literally everything in your life works better with this alignment.

Grounding . . . Coming Home To Your *Self*

Grounding is not just an intellectual, analytical experience. Rather it is a visceral full-body experience integrating all aspects of your self with a connection to the energies of the physical Earth. If your physical body is energetically connected into the physical Earth, all your interactions with the 3rd dimension are changed somehow and lived from a completely different perspective.

When you think of a Grounded person, you usually think of someone who exudes a power that gives them self-control, of being present in a pragmatic and focused way. Their life seems to have more flow, clear communication and they're able to manifest their goals. Grounded people seem to manage their affairs in an efficient, intelligent way and are usually successful people.

When I first began my work as a clairvoyant, I'd frequently hear my clients ask me this question, "What is my life's purpose?" Often times, I'd hear my intuitive voice inside my mind respond, "You just need to get here!" I became aware of how so many people's conscious awareness was not part of their everyday lives.

Chapter 1: What Is Grounding?

There seemed to be a fundamental connection where too many people were lacking focus or were too traumatized to be completely present and engaged with life.
Usually, these were well-intentioned, well-meaning people living their lives without a good foundation or in certain instances, with no foundation, nor the full commitment required to manifest their goals and fulfill their dreams. Their life was full of hard work, which generally they were willing to do, but they weren't particularly productive or successful.

Another way to define Grounding is as an energetic connection that anchors and secures your personal life force energy to the life force energy of the Earth. Just as the force of gravity draws everything toward the very center of the Earth, your conscious alignment with the power of the Earth gives your life a sense of presence and magnitude of being an extension of the forces of nature where everything is facilitated. This empowering, nurturing quality fosters a sense of synchronicity in your life, of being in the right place and very present in now time. This is your most fundamental connection for being human.

Grounding... Coming Home To Your *Self*

If your personal grounding connection is intact, than your primary relationship to your Self is connected into the supportive energies of nature. As this alliance is forged, life seems to flow with more grace and ease. And, if your primary relationship to your Self is strengthened and balanced then your relationships with others are more harmonious, appropriate and balanced as well.

The demeanor of a Grounded person is saying, "I am present and accounted for! I am sovereign. I am fully responsible and in-charge of my life! I am consciously creating the life I want." This incredible journey all begins with a simple Grounding visualization. At first you have to consciously make the effort until this Grounding process takes on a life of its own. Then it becomes a natural extension of who you are.

I'll be your guide in increasing your awareness as we journey to the center of the Earth. I'll share with you many of my own experiences and observations, and much of the wisdom I've gathered along this path. Grounding will make your present life experience more worth living. It will stabilize your energies as you

Chapter 1: What Is Grounding?

evolve through these unprecedented times of change. We need as many Grounded people as possible on the planet. Grounding will help you navigate through these uncertain times with more confidence and stability. It will support you in creating and actualizing your vision for your personal life and for the world.

A Simple Grounding Meditation...

Grounding is the most basic and powerful healing technique for you to become aware of and to integrate in your daily life. With the use of a visualization technique, you create an energetic connection from your physical body into the physical Earth. The visualization is a direct, straight extension from the base of your spine, deep down into the core of the Earth. When done properly, this creates an electrical frequency or current of energy through the body, which many people can actually feel. Think of all the electrical appliances in your house, in order for them to function properly, they all have a Grounding wire. Without it, the appliance would short circuit, smoke, spark and not work properly. In order for our bodies and our lives to function, humans need a type of Grounding connection as well.

Grounding ... Coming Home To Your *Self*

All forms of meditation usually begin with a centering technique, such as a conscious awareness of being in your own body, listening to your breath, or hearing the sound of your own heart beating. These things help a person consciously and deliberately gather all fragments of their consciousness to be fully in the Now, which is the basic theme for Grounding. Throughout this book, there'll be several guided meditations to help you. Each one of them is a form of centering process, Grounding and healing.

First, there are many ways to visualize the Grounding Cord. Here's a very simple Grounding Meditation that's a good beginning point:

- Take a deep breath and bring your attention and focus inside your body.
- Listen to the sound of your breath and allow your body to relax and feel calm.
- Bring your attention to the base of your spine.
- Imagine that your tailbone becomes a taproot, like the main root of a tree that extends deep down into the core of the Earth. This is your Grounding Cord. Some people perceive their Grounding Cord as a

Chapter 1: What Is Grounding?

cylinder or light beam that extends from your spine down into the core of the Earth. Whatever symbol provides a measure of comfort for you is fine.
- As you reach the core of the Earth, simply spend time in this place and get a feeling or a sense of the quality of Earth energy. You may experience this place as an image, picture, symbol or emotional state. You might see a color, or get a feeling or sensation.
- Feel the consistency of the Earth energies and attune your personal energies with the Earth.
- Spend some time getting better acquainted with the Earth essence energy as your new best friend. Take a breath and relax into this sensation.
- Hold this position for as long as is comfortable—5 minutes is a good starting place or begin with 1 to 2 minutes if that's more comfortable. Affirm that you want to maintain this Grounded energetic connection for 1 hour or for 2 hours, or throughout your day. If this is your intention, the energy in your body will make this so.
- Know that every effort you make to Ground is building psychic muscle mass to a sustaining Grounding connection that you have all the time.

Grounding . . . Coming Home To Your *Self*

Some people simply love the experience of Grounding because it can be fun and it generally feels good. Some report sensations of warmth and even states of bliss. Your Grounding Cord is the foundation for your life and is tangential to everything you do.

Here's what some people had to say regarding their Grounding experience:

I felt my heart open up. My Grounding made a subtle shift, but there was a sense that everything was balanced and fine. Earth energy does feel like unconditional mother love energy. If ever I begin to feel alone or disconnected, Grounding helps me to feel better. It's very nurturing and reassuring. If ever I find myself feeling nervous and insecure, I find Grounding helps me to be calm and relaxed, so I can handle more expanded states of consciousness in my everyday life.

I Grounded into the center of the Earth and brought gold energy up through my Grounding. It felt very warm and even blissful, so that was wonderful. The other times I had a little trouble doing it; I didn't know why, but generally I would simply relax and sink into

Chapter 1: What Is Grounding?

it and it seemed to work better. I think the relaxation helps tremendously. If I'm tense, it's a little tough to feel Grounded. Whenever I allow the force of gravity to take my Grounding and just anchor then I usually have better success.

As I felt my connection to the Earth, I noticed an energy shift inside me. It started out as a very dense, flat matte, red color, and that changed into various colors. It was very beautiful and felt wonderful.

Grounding and Self-Healing Meditation

Even though Grounding in itself is very healing, you can expand the Grounding process specifically for healing your own personal issues. If there are negative conditions in your body or emotions that keep you from being comfortable, or at peace with yourself, try the following technique to help you manage those states. Who doesn't need healing from time to time?

- Sit in a comfortable place.
- Take a deep breath and come to a relaxing feeling of serenity in your body. Listen to the sound of your own heartbeat and quiet your mind.

Grounding . . . Coming Home To Your *Self*

- Listen to the sound of your breath. Allow all your body systems to slow down.
- Bring your awareness to the base of your spine.
- Extend your Grounding Cord into the Earth's core. Imagine that the core of the Earth is a large pool of liquid 24K Gold.
- Ground into the center of the pool of Liquid Gold and simply feel this connection.
- Visualize that your Grounding Cord is a giant honey spoon stirring the Liquid Gold energy. Feel a visceral sense of this frequency and feel comfort with this healing Earth energy.
- Imagine that your Grounding Cord is a giant drinking straw. Begin to draw the Liquid Gold energy into your body simply with the power of your mind and intention.
- Allow this energy to flow throughout your body, through your pelvis area—washing away any discordant energies, allow these energies to wash through your reproductive system and elimination system to dissolve any negativity there. Bring these energies up higher to your mid-section and chest areas clearing all the major organs in your body affirming that they can function at top

Chapter 1: What Is Grounding?

efficiency. Clear any stress, constriction, discomfort or invalidation messages or any aspect of yourself that feels less than loving and continue to the area of your head, to your throat, front and back. Visualize sending this energy though your arms and legs and down your Grounding Cord again.
- Check again to see if there's a place of tension anywhere in your body, affirm that you are directing this flow of energy to that part of your body and allow it to permeate through that space. You may notice that the parts within you where this energy has been feel different somehow—perhaps more relaxed, open, free and clear. Yes?
- When your body feels saturated with gold, reground and completely be sure that you've filled your entire body to full capacity with this Earth gold. Be sure not leave any open spaces or unfilled areas as the human body doesn't like emptiness. So affirm to yourself that every cell, every sub atomic particle within you is saturated with these healing energies and will continue for the next 24 hours.
- Take a deep breath and affirm that you want to live your life from a Grounded place where you're naturally bathed in healing energy all the time.

Grounding ... Coming Home To Your *Self*

The human body loves gold. This is a simple meditation with Earth energy that makes you feel good to be inside your own skin. It heals, clears old dysfunctional energy, it lightens the load of density so you feel lighter and happier. Here are some experiences from other people doing this Grounding and healing process:

As I brought the gold Earth energies into my Grounding it was as if the knots began letting go. At first, the Grounding resembled a muscle cramp then it began releasing. The very first thing I noticed was this amazing relaxation of my body. The more I cleared, the more peace and calm I felt. I feel like my Grounding Cord is clear and very filled with light and there is color coming from the Earth.

The Grounding Meditation was so powerful. My cat who never bothers me, is sitting here on my lap. He was really attracted to the Grounding process I was doing. It was wonderful feeling the Earth energy flowing through me as a sparkly, brilliant red, orange and gold. Oh, I had so much garbage in me that I just kept giving it to the Earth. And I noticed a much needed clearing from my throat, and I could feel my sexual

Chapter 1: What Is Grounding?

center definitely waking up. I could feel those sparkles all down my legs. it's been on the back shelf a long time. So I think I'm rejuvenating those parts of myself as I Ground.

Grounding . . . Coming Home To Your *Self*

Chapter 2
Keeping it Simple

I decided a long time ago that I'd always approach Grounding with a sense of freshness and newness as if I were constantly Grounding for the first time. This approach was more intelligent than I realized as I'm often shown new and different ways to Ground. The stability that Grounding provides is especially important for these changing times when the events of our lives seem to be moving faster than we can manage.

My relationship to the Earth is constantly teaching me and presenting me with new and different perceptions. Even though I've been Grounding for almost 30 years, I've always approached this process with the openness, simplicity, curiosity and wonder of a child. By keeping my Earth connection fresh, fluid and open, this demeanor is the perfect modality for spontaneous learning and a deepening relationship with the Earth to occur. Grounding also makes my physical body feel comfortable and pleasant in an integrated way.

The Journey Begins...

When I was younger, I had two occupations. I worked as a nurse and taught elementary school children, although never at the same time. Usually I worked as a nurse until I became tired of the hospital scene then I'd change occupations and work as an elementary school teacher. Back and forth and so my life would go...

Having always been sensitive, it seemed that everything in the world was overwhelming to me. I initially thought this was due to my having chosen two of the most stressful occupations one can have. I was young and healthy, always had more energy than I knew what to do with, and had an innate sense of wanting to help people.

Chapter 2: Keeping it Simple

In the midst of my very busy life as a school teacher, I began a Clairvoyant Training Program on the recommendation of a psychic. The psychic advised me of my need to establish better boundaries between myself and other people. She said, "You have all this energy in and around you that has nothing to do with who you are. You need to stop taking on the issues of the people you work with." I said, "So what should I do?" What she then advised me was the absolute last thing I ever expected. She said, "You need to learn to be a psychic!" "And what's THAT supposed to do?" I said in utter disbelief. How did learning to be clairvoyant have anything to do with establishing boundaries? I didn't know at the time, but I have come to appreciate the wisdom of her advice over the years.

The study of clairvoyance taught me autonomy and the importance of keeping my energy field clear. What a good feeling that is! With this new awareness, I established a better sense of who I am and what my personal energies feel like for the first time in my life. As I was growing up, I was extremely sensitive with innate empathic abilities without a clue as to how to manage those gifts and no one to guide me. As a result, over time I'd become inundated with other people's issues and energies, how was I to know who I was or how I was supposed to feel? As I learned to clear my field and gather my energies and to Ground, I realized the importance of being and feeling clear and sovereign. It changed my life and made a huge difference in my personal happiness, self-expression, clarity and peace of mind.

Grounding in the Classroom

I was teaching 4th grade, my favorite age group, when I began my studies to become a Clairvoyant. I would teach children by day and do Clairvoyant training a couple of nights per week. Children are really good barometers for whatever happens to be the state of your life. They reflect your state of mind. It seemed if I was in a calm state, the children were calm. If I was stressed, the children exhibited all types of stressful behavior to contend with affecting them and me as their teacher.

My clairvoyant instructor talked about the Grounding process and described symptoms of when a person is

Chapter 2: Keeping it Simple

Grounded and when a person is ungrounded. I could certainly relate to the list. "When a person is Grounded," she said, "communication is more clear and direct. Other people are generally able to better hear the true message of what you are saying." So I decided to practice being Grounded in an elementary classroom situation and notice the results.

My 4th graders were my barometers for what I was learning in Clairvoyant training. This was my own personal independent research for how well this clairvoyant training was working in the real world. We all know how common it is for children to space out and daydream during class time, but when I spoke in front of the class from a Grounded place, I seemed to be able to hold the attention of all 30 children. To my amazement, I remember thinking, "The children are listening to me!" This was unbelievable, wonderful and astonishing! How could something so simple be so effective? I noticed that even the sound, tone and quality of my voice was different and more compelling to them.

Since that went so well, I decided to teach Grounding to my 4th grade class. When they returned to the

Grounding . . . Coming Home To Your *Self*

classroom from recess, I'd say, "If you left any parts of yourself on the playground, call them back into your self so that ALL of you is here and comfortably seated at your desk. Close your eyes and imagine that you are a tree growing roots into the Earth and that you are aware of how your whole body feels as your are seated at your desk. Notice the roots going down and loving the rich soil and all the good feelings that come from your roots connecting into the Earth."

The children loved these exercises. When we spent time doing this, I noticed that the rest of the day went more smoothly. I found the children to be more focused and ready for their studies. Grounding facilitates learning of all topics—not just in class, but also in life. I was amazed. My job as a 4th grade classroom teacher was facilitated and worked beautifully with these simple exercises. And, it seemed that the children enjoyed feeling more centered and present in their bodies. What a nice addition to the classroom situation!

Chapter 3
The Benefits of Grounding

The advantages to Grounding are extensive. I suggest you practice reading this chapter from a Grounded place. Simply bring your focus and attention to your Grounding and affirm that you will be anchored into the Earth for the duration of reading this chapter. It's good to include exercises like this throughout the day as it strengthens your commitment and your body's ability to Ground. Here are some of the more obvious reasons for living a Grounded life:

Grounding makes you feel more centered, alert and aware with presence of mind. With Grounding, there's more of a commitment to be present and to participate more fully in life from this very empowered, clear-thinking, take-charge state. It very simply makes you feel more awake, aware and engaged with your life.

Grounding facilitates synchronicity in life. Synchronicity is the simultaneous occurrence of events that appear related but have no discernible connection. We sometimes refer to this as "being in the right place at the right time," when two or more seemingly unrelated events come together in a way that almost appears magical. A common example is when we think of a person and have an unexpected encounter with them later in the day. With Grounding, more connecting points are established to create a seemingly magical synchronistic existence.

Health, focus, clarity and harmony of your mind and body are facilitated as Grounding brings all aspects of your self into a unified state. This allows your life-force energies to flow in a more even distribution throughout your system creating feelings of relaxation, calm certainty, confidence and synchronicity. The mind and physical body functions beautifully coalesce into a unified alignment bringing everything into harmo-

Chapter 3: The Benefits of Grounding

ny. Being in 50 different fragmented stressful states cannot occur when one is properly Grounded.

Once energy Grounding is established, it creates a state of neutrality in your consciousness where you're centered and clear. Grounding brings all aspects of the self in a unified state, where we truly get our lives together. From this place, we become neutral and able to view the extremes and emotional states of others without being at the effect. People report feeling more secure, confident, empowered and less affected by the trauma/drama of daily life. Being anchored in a centered, empowered, neutral place, allows you to be in that state and stay there no matter what is happening around you. What a gift that is!

Grounding assists you in communicating clearly with confidence, truth and in a compelling way. In the second chapter, I shared with you my personal Grounding experience as a 4th grade classroom teacher. The children were listening to me because they could feel my communication came from a very empowered Grounded place. I communicated in a way that compelled a classroom of 30 children of ages 9 to 10 years old to give me their full attention! This works with children and it works in your communication with people of all ages.

Being centered and Grounded in your body puts you in a constant state of emotional healing and awareness. Being at one with the healing energies of the Earth constantly washing through you is like being bathed in healing energies all day long. As your Grounding becomes a natural part of who you are, the healing energies pulse through your system generating a 24/7 system of Earth healing energies for you at all times.

Grounding allows for an opening of your perceptive abilities. This is specifically why psychics and clairvoyants learn the Grounding process first. The more you Ground you may notice that your intuition is clearer, open, controlled with information naturally flowing through your consciousness with grace and ease. Intuition, clear perception and Grounding are extremely useful in all occupations.

Grounding strengthens and nourishes your entire central nervous system. The union of the human body with the Earth creates an electrical

Chapter 3: The Benefits of Grounding

current that courses through your physiology and makes everything function better, in a healthy sense. Many people report that they can actually feel this current flowing through them, which nourishes and replenishes the human system with life-force and facilitates good health for the body and mind.

Grounding strengthens your aura and creates energetic protection, which is another reason why energy healers generally learn a Grounding technique first. In all forms of energy healing, energetic protection is an extremely important aspect of this work. Grounding greatly affects the entire aura, which is the energy field surrounding the physical body. Grounding makes the aura more dense, but in a more refined way. People with a light, ethereal quality to their aura, have a tendency to feel overwhelmed and bombarded by life or by the energies of others converging in their field. A person with this type of constitution may experience life as unbearable, intolerable, and even miserable. The practice of Grounding on a regular basis will strengthen the protective energies surrounding the physical body and improve this issue for them incrementally over time. In this world, during these times, who doesn't need more psychic energetic protection?

Grounding reinforces your immunity making you less susceptible to colds and flu. When Grounding occurs, the aura is reinforced. When the aura is reinforced, it protects you from all these types of influences not conducive to the health of your mind and body.

People who work near electronic equipment need Grounding. Have you had moments in life when no matter what you did, your computer or other electronic equipment refused to function properly? It's not uncommon for the electrical energies in the body of an ungrounded person to trigger electronic equipment to function in all kinds of bizarre ways. The physical body is quite electrical and needs a good solid Grounding connection to function properly. With Grounding, the health of your body is managed as well as the functionality of electronic equipment in your environment.

Chapter 3: The Benefits of Grounding

Grounding helps you to manifest and actualize your goals. Once, while teaching a clairvoyant training class, I asked my students to psychically assess the Grounding Cords of Bill Gates, Oprah Winfrey and Donald Trump. Everyone reported that they were profoundly Grounded, dynamic and fearless. These influential leaders readily actualize goals that impact lives all over the world. They are our mentors for how to be Grounded to generate creative ideas that then get fully manifested into reality. When you Ground your physical body into the physical Earth, this is like dancing with your favorite dance partner. Your personal energies intermingle with the Earth energies consciously co-creating for yourself the life you want that is supportive, sustaining, creative and extending success to all your endeavors.

Grounding allows you to release blocks, stress and unwanted energy. Your Grounding Cord naturally drains unhealthy and unwanted stressful, dysfunctional energies from your physical and emotional bodies while you're constantly connected into the Earth. This nice feature alone is worth taking the time to learn Grounding! People who are ungrounded

Grounding . . . Coming Home To Your *Self*

don't get to release the stress, blocks and dysfunctional energy. Instead, these negative states accumulate in their energy anatomy, which contributes to a long litany of problems over time. With the added psychic weight, this can actually create physical weight gain. These ungrounded states rarely contribute to people feeling happy, peaceful, confident or fulfilled. Grounding is so important for our fundamental happiness and peace of mind.

Grounding empowers you to manage much of your personal process. If you learn some simple healing techniques through your Grounding Cord, much of the density in your field can be cleared. This allows you to keep your energy field clear and to be completely in charge of your own self-healing and ultimately your life.

Grounding enhances creativity and all forms of artistic expression. Many artists, writers, dancers, musicians, and people using different creative modalities use Grounding to experience greater artistic ideas, expression and sustained creativity. As you Ground, not only intuition and the world of images and symbols are

Chapter 3: The Benefits of Grounding

activated, but creativity and inspiration is enhanced as well. This stimulates the creative part of your brain to work in concert with the linear side. When creativity is sparked, people become naturally absorbed in the creative process, which aligns the spirit and body. Appreciate the wonder of so many works of art born from this state. Works of art often remind us of the spirit residing within each of us inspiring beauty and creativity. So many remarkable aspects of human expression are integrated and brought into wholeness through Grounding.

You experience your physical body from a healthier and more enjoyable place. Being Grounded means being in your body and living your life to the fullest. We see this state in an athlete's ability to have fluidity, agility, and be masterful at sports. Think of a time when your body was healthy and you enjoyed being in it. Be grateful for the gift of a strong, healthy body.

Athletes who include Grounding as part of their daily routine report feeling more integrated and have better performance. Most athletes are very naturally Grounded people. As spectators, you watch their performances often times in awe of their skill, ability and sheer presence of mind. You appreciate and enjoy the total commitment they bring to the game. The Creator gave us bodies and they know what to do with them. The next time you watch a game of any sport, take a moment to enjoy the Grounding presence of these professional athletes. Learn from these athletes! Activate as much of that sense of Grounding into robust good health that you can bring to your personal life.

Grounding and Tennis

Once I had a boyfriend named Julian and one of the things we loved to do on weekends was play a few games of tennis. As we began playing tennis together, I knew more about the game then he did only to have his abilities quickly surpass my own. After a while, I quite frankly grew tired of losing to this guy.

I decided to bring my Grounding cord to the tennis court. Each time before I served, I quickly brought my attention to my Grounding connection, anchoring it, reaffirming it, securing it, and then I'd serve the ball.

Chapter 3: The Benefits of Grounding

What I didn't expect was no matter how I served the ball, Julian was unable to score a point, or sometimes even hit the ball at all. I was confident that Grounding would help my game. But I was both amazed and perplexed at the effects it had on my partner!?!

I was finally on a winning streak as Julian became noticeably bothered by his losing streak. I heard the frustration in his voice as he called to me from the other side of the court, "How come every time you hit the ball, I feel like something mystical is happening?" "Well," I said, "I am a mystic, is it so unusual that I bring my mystical abilities to the tennis game?"

I finally shared with him my newly found success in tennis. He asked me all about Grounding and I even taught him how to Ground. He practiced the simple technique and found it totally helped his tennis game. That unfortunately marked the end of my winning streak. However, both our tennis games improved and it changed the nature of our relating to one another. We shared the wins and losses. Good for our game, good for morale and good for our relationship.

Grounding . . . Coming Home To Your *Self*

Chapter 4
Helpful Hints ...

Here are suggestions to help you Ground more easily:

- Keep it simple, be comfortable, keep your body in a state of ease and balance
- Take several deep breaths to help you get in your body. Breathing slows down all the body functions, stills and quiets the mind, helps you to focus and brings all aspects of yourself together. So remember to ... breathe...
- Being relaxed is important or try to center as much as you can
- Don't willfully or mentally force your Grounding. This is like using brute force or will power, which may Ground your mental body, but not all aspects of you. Remember to take care of all aspects of your self.

Grounding ... Coming Home To Your *Self*

- Practice makes perfect. Practice the simple Grounding technique every day or several times a day.
- Create a personal routine to help you remember to Ground daily. For example, Ground every hour on the hour, or every time the phone rings.
- Design your own daily reminder or Grounding Meditation for yourself as an affirmation, visualization, feeling or emotion. As you begin to Ground, there are many simple ways to incorporate this in your daily life. If you're a visual person, you may "see" your Grounding as a symbol, such as a tree root or another personal symbol that you consciously use as a visual to remind yourself to be Grounded. Find a symbol that feels right and comfortable for you and use it to reinforce your Grounding. People who aren't particularly visual may use a simple, effective affirmation, "I am now completely Grounded in present time." Some people may have a feeling or emotional sense of stability, wholeness and wellness to remind them to be Grounded. When they become ungrounded, they conjure that feeling to restore the Grounding connection. Once this becomes a habit, Grounding

becomes a natural expression of who you are and how you feel all the time.
- As much as possible, clear your mind of all the cares of your life and be comfortable with states of simply being with yourself
- Practice Dr. Liu's Chi Gong Exercise for Stress.

Dr. Liu's Chi Gong Exercise for Stress

I've had the pleasure of knowing a phenomenal yet eccentric Chinese herbalist and acupuncturist named Dr. Johannes Liu of Seattle, Washington. Dr. Liu was distinguished as the finest Chinese herbalist in the state of Washington by the medical community. I witnessed more miracles through the work of Dr. Liu, than anyone else I've ever known.

Dr. Liu was short-tempered, commanding, incisive, and opinionated. He didn't like unconscious people and strongly disliked the proverbial "Ugly American" asking him too many questions. The "Ugly American" is a stereotype that gives Americans a bad reputation around the world as the one who is loud, arrogant, demeaning, thoughtless, incapable of being sensitive to people of other cultures and judging everything by American standards.

Dr. Liu usually threw these people out of his office without any explanation. "Out!" he'd say, "Get Out!" If you swallowed your pride and re-scheduled to see him again after such a rude experience, it was as if he never remembered the incident. In fact, Dr. Liu never seemed to remember any of his patients at all! Each visit was just like the first. I referred many people to Dr. Liu as he completely cured their conditions by the powerful and specific Chinese herbal remedies that he combined for just the right effect. Dr. Liu charged $30 per visit, which included 3 small bags of these magnificent Chinese herbs that seemed to cure just about anything!

I loved knowing Dr. Liu and his unconventional style with people and even his abrupt ways were refreshing, as you definitely knew where you stood with him. He was the quintessential healer whom I admired and respected. He's retired now, but his life's work was an admirable contribution to those who had the good fortune to experience his genius.
One of the most valuable things Dr. Liu taught me

Chapter 4: Helpful Hints for Grounding ...

was a simple Chi Gong exercise for stress. In his very limited English with heavy Chinese accent, he referred to this exercise as—the "Chi Gong Exercise for Stress." I asked, "Dr. Liu, for how long should one do the exercise?" In typical Dr. Liu style, he abruptly responded, "Not 'how long,' you just DO!"

I discovered that the Chi Gong Exercise for Stress was incredibly helpful to experience being in one's body in a healing way as it opened many of the meridians flushing life force energy throughout the body. I couldn't help but notice that the Chi Gong Exercise for Stress was the most excellent precursor to being more Grounded. I found it to be so helpful that it soon became the first thing I taught my students in my Grounding classes. Moreover, it was perfect for managing the body of stress, which is the foundation for 80 to 90% of all disease. Here's the process:

- From a seated position with your feet flat on the floor, back straight, place the outer edge of your hands on your lap.
- Simply be in a relaxed position. You may begin to feel pulsing, tingling and relaxation. Your whole

Grounding . . . Coming Home To Your *Self*

body relaxes the longer you hold this posture.

This simple exercise can be done while watching TV, talking on the phone with a headset, sitting in class, sitting at a restaurant waiting for the waiter to bring your order, visiting with a friend, or simply sitting quietly and feeling the wonderful effects of this simple exercise. It's easy, it's palpable, it feels great, it reduces stress and helps you be comfortable in your own body.

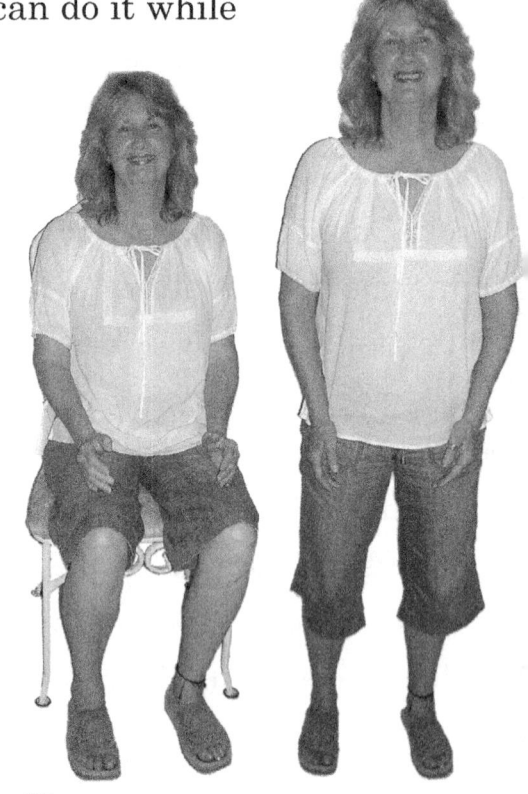

At right are illustrations of the Chi Gong Exercise for Stress. You can do it while seated in a chair as shown in the first illustration. You can also do it standing up. And, if ever you have a difficult time getting to sleep, you can also hold the same hand posture while lying down. The deep relaxation you feel from this Chi Gong posture will quiet your mind and make you feel peaceful until you naturally fall asleep.

With Dr. Liu's Chi Gong Exercise for Stress, try another Grounding Meditation with the healing energy of the Earth permeating throughout your physical body...Enjoy!

Grounding Meditation with Dr. Liu's Chi Gong Exercise for Stress

- Sit in a chair, feet flat on the floor with the outer aspect of your hands resting comfortably on your lap as shown in the illustration of Dr. Liu's Chi Gong Exercise for Stress.
- Take a deep breath and come to a relaxing feeling inside your own body.
- Listen to the sound of your breath. Bring your awareness to the base of your spine.
- You may notice a tingling in your legs and arms or different parts of your body. This is an increase of life-force energy flowing through your body and is very beneficial and nurturing for health and management of stress.

Grounding ... Coming Home To Your *Self*

- Extend your Grounding Cord into the Earth's core and be aware that your Earth connection may be deeper than before. The Chi Gong exercise is very beneficial for learning how to Ground.
- The longer you sit in this posture in the Chi Gong pose and consciously Ground, the better you experience the power of this process.
- Hold this posture for as long as is comfortable. The longer you maintain the Grounding and the Chi Gong Exercise for Stress pose, the more it opens the meridians creating an infusion of life-force energy throughout your body. Should you notice pain or discomfort anywhere in your body, this is usually an indicator of a blockage working its way out of your system. Take a few relaxing deep breaths to facilitate the clearing.
- The longer you hold the pose, the more it dissipates energy blocks. But take this slowly, and do this a few times a day or whenever you think about it.
- Take a deep breath and affirm for yourself feelings of well-being, health, vitality, Grounded with life force energy flowing through your body at all times!

Chapter 4: Helpful Hints for Grounding ...

Suggestions when Grounding is Difficult

Not all initial Grounding experiences are beautiful, however. There are times when Grounding can activate feelings of discomfort when you begin the process as issues that kept you from being Grounded begin to make their presence known. Just breathe and relax and try to consciously push through this, until you feel more balanced. It could be that people who have had many challenges in life need much more than a few deep breaths to better Ground. At this stage, it's important to increase your awareness of Grounding and to keep it simple and light and be very respectful of what your body can comfortably do.

Some activities that help your Grounding are anything that makes your body feel good. Outdoor activities or simply being out in nature can enhance your Grounding experience. Any hobby, commitment or interest that engages your attention, relaxes your body, helps you to focus, makes you happy and requires your full participation helps you to Ground.

Grounding... Coming Home To Your *Self*

Mothers and fathers are instinctively present and Grounded due to the love and responsibility they instinctively feel to care for their children. Other people are committed to their work, which compels a person's mental cohesiveness, focus and dedication and contributes to the presence of mind we often experience in Grounded people. So involve yourself in activities that you love to do and this alone will feed your spirit and assist your ability to be happily present and fully engaged in your personal life.

People inherently feel the healing power of nature, which replenishes life force and good feelings igniting the desire to be more aligned in life. Outdoor activities engaging the element of nature are a wonderful precursor for Grounding. Here's a list of these and you can probably add some activities of your own that you enjoy:

- Hiking
- Dancing (indoor or out)
- Biking
- Sports
- Gardening
- Walking barefoot on the ground

Chapter 4: Helpful Hints for Grounding ...

- Camping
- Literally any outdoor activities
- Art
- Hobbies we enjoy
- Creative endeavors
- Doing things we love

Situations when you really need Grounding...

- Whenever you feel clumsy, spacey, forgetful, ungrounded, vulnerable
- Whenever you feel sad or depressed
- Whenever you feel disconnected from everything and everybody
- Whenever you feel anxious or you're in stressful situations
- Whenever you need to give a presentation, lecture or performance
- When working near electronic equipment
- During the onset of a cold, flu or other illness
- Before and during physical exercise
- At bedtime, before you fall asleep
- Throughout any busy workday

Suggestions when Grounding feels Impossible

Some people Ground and report feelings of discomfort as though being in their body on Earth is challenging if not impossible. It could be that your experience in life was or is traumatic. These discomforts and traumatic memories surface into conscious awareness when they Ground. Do not be afraid of this! Instead, see this as one of these "wonderful opportunities for your personal growth." If you push through these undesirable states while learning to Ground, much of this negativity will go into the Earth where it gets instantly neutralized. At first, this requires trust, perhaps some courage and some practice. But once you understand the process, it facilitates your personal growth while you learn to manage undesirable emotional states and transform them into more presence of mind, inner peace and stability.

What are some of these negative emotional states? Fear, anger, shock, jealousy, unwanted memories from the past, all forms of dysfunction, co-dependency, power blocks, obstacles, limitations, trauma, abuse of all kinds, lack or poverty consciousness, the list goes on and on...

Chapter 4: Helpful Hints for Grounding ...

The reasons why people are ungrounded are numerous. It's usually due to negative experiences, abuse, and an unfortunate long list of reasons why people can't seem to get in their bodies, enjoy a fundamental connection with the Earth and have meaningful lives.

In addition, there is a history of many old, negative thought-forms on the planet that are anything but hospitable, calming, nurturing or loving. Some of these haunt humanity making a connection to Earth energies arduous or a horrible experience. These are usually associated with war, hardship and misery reminiscent with dark periods of Earth's history, belief systems, or superstitions, or any connotation that hell, fire and brimstone exist down within the Earth.

If Grounding ever becomes difficult, simply take a deep breath, try relaxing, and moving beyond these kinds of thought-forms into the Grounding experience. Simply allow your self to see these types of falsity for what they are and move beyond them to states that support empowering and loving thoughts and feelings. If however, for all you try on your own, you're unable to Ground, then you might consider getting some help.

Grounding... Coming Home To Your *Self*

Old negative psychological issues can become energetically calcified in your energy anatomy over time and make it impossible to Ground. Feeling stuck in old patterns can be a hardship, so get some help to manage this. If you clear these energies, it'll be easier for you to experience your Grounding Cord and begin feeling supported, happy, healed and shifting your life to a better, more functional place. Then you'll be able to perform more of the Grounding Meditations on your own from a much more comfortable place.

The following are suggestions for when Grounding seems really, really difficult:

- Seek a gifted healer or therapist who understands these issues and can help you resolve the source of your problems
- Massage is instrumental at clearing the abusive memory patterns out of your body so find a good massage therapist
- Get a gentle structural adjustment from a competent chiropractor
- Work with a counselor whom you feel comfortable with and has good counseling skills

Chapter 4: Helpful Hints for Grounding ...

- See a reputable homeopath
- See an understanding doctor and take medication for a while if you need to
- In essence, draw on the expertise of anyone who can assist you in clearing the energy blocks or the backlog of emotional issues that may have become lodged in your body and psyche.

Clearing, healing, resolving the backlog of memory imprints that were difficult helps unload psychic and emotional density. It lightens our heavy burdens. In so doing, Grounding is greatly facilitated. Don't ever become discouraged by what has happened to you in the past. These things become imprinted in the psyche as energy and they can be changed. In the following chapters, you'll learn how to do these types of energy clearings for yourself. You'll be amazed that you can do much of your own clearings very simply. But should the process ever become overwhelming, remember to get support and assistance from someone who can help you.

Grounding . . . Coming Home To Your *Self*

Chapter 5
Refining Grounding

The "Practice Makes Perfect" advice is really true. For it is in the moments of actually doing this work, that you truly learn and have more and more moments of connecting to this information and making it your very own. As your body understands how invaluable it feels to be in your own space in a more profound way, you begin to relax, and experience melding into the flow of life.

As you Ground, you may get impressions or even begin to visualize a color or colors, a symbol, a mental picture or a feeling sensation. Since Grounding is the first thing that a clairvoyant learns to manage their perceptive abilities, you may begin to have quick mental images or pictures spontaneously come into your mind. This is the beginning phase for how a clairvoyant learns to perceive energy and then deciphers what all the imagery means. In truth, you'll come to realize that you're psychic and that we're all psychic and you get intuitive impressions, mental images and pictures in your mind all the time!

Visuals for your Grounding Cord...

You can work with symbols to help your Grounding experience. Every one has a Grounding Cord or should and this can be visualized by a symbol, which is limited only by your imagination. In choosing a symbol that will represent your Grounding connection, you want to select one that is comfortable and feels balanced and reassuring to you personally. This is a very individual process. If you work with a symbol and it's not quite right, change it until you find the right fit. What's important to remember is that your Grounding Cord needs to be an extension from your physical body all the way into the physical Earth with a complete connection in between.

Chapter 5: Refining Grounding

Years ago, I taught a Grounding class with 13 beautiful young women in their 20's and 30's. It was a wonderful experience for us all to explore the realms of Grounding together. I asked them to first visualize their Grounding Cords in a guided meditation and then sketch their Grounding Cords, color them and talk about them. One young mother's Grounding Cord was a very detailed giant umbilical cord extended from her perineum to the core of the Earth. It was one of the most profound renditions of a Grounding Cord I'd ever seen. Here are others that people report seeing. So hopefully these will spark ideas for your own Grounding Cord:

- A column of light connecting the base of your spine into the Earth
- A cylinder about 3-4 inches wide extending from your perineum to the Earth's core
- Your tailbone turns into a giant root and grows deep down and connects into the Earth's core
- A waterfall
- A rope
- Rebar or a steel cable
- A vine
- A taproot

Visualizing Earth Energy...

Your relationship to the energies of the Earth will become more firmly established and clear as you Ground. You may experience this as a feeling, a sensation, a symbol, a color, a smell. It's good to qualify how the Earth energies feel to you as this sharpens your Grounding experience and helps you become more conscious and aware of the biggest and best support system you've ever had—the Earth. As you access this state, you'll be mindful of the power and the healing energies that are available to you whenever you turn your attention to the Earth. Here are a few descriptions for how the energy of the Earth makes people feel.

- A maternal unconditional love energy...
- A bright sun—such as the molten core of the Earth
- Seeing Earth energy as a beautiful woman
- Gorgeous and bold colors
- Fecund smell of the Earth
- A constant, powerful force that supports and sustains
- The source of Creation energy in all things

Chapter 5: Refining Grounding

- A wellspring of healing energy for the body, emotions, mind, and spirit

One student shared her grounding experience in the following way:
"As I Grounded into the Earth, the healing energies opened to me and I felt connected, embraced, loved, accepted and that comforted me very much."

Grounding Sensations...

As you Ground, you may experience that your body will feel differently. The act of Grounding nourishes the entire central nervous system that changes the electrical currents in the body. This supports you to be more integrated in your sense of self. It opens your perceptions so you can see more clearly and in a more expanded perspective. Being Grounded establishes a connection to the essence of the Earth that is constantly healing the body, emotions and all aspects of the self 24 hours a day, 7 days a week.
What does a healing feel like? How do you know when you're being healed? Simply tune into your body and be aware of how you feel. What impressions or physi-

cal body sensations are you getting? The most common symptoms and descriptions for how it feels to be Grounded into the Earth experiencing healing energies are:

- The body is more relaxed
- A palpable warmth and current of energy flowing through body
- Pulsing, tingling sensations throughout your body
- A feeling of density, that's refined and more committed to the physical realm
- Physical vision and perception have more clarity
- Feeling more expanded and powerful
- Balanced
- A feeling of neutrality
- Confident
- Stronger levels of personal power and energy
- A feeling of oneness with nature and everything

Symptoms of blocks and discordant energies in the body

With the varieties of discordant and disharmony energies in our lives, it's not uncommon to find any num-

Chapter 5: Refining Grounding

ber of these in your energy field. The process of Grounding and your intention to clear these unwanted states automatically begins the clearing process, which is wonderful. You may be aware of these negative energies leaving your body, which may sometimes stress a person as they see or feel these old issues or memories. But no worries, these issues are passing through your conscious awareness as it vacates your energy field—it's actually leaving. But instead of seeing these moments as sign of relief, often times, people mistakenly think the old traumas and abuse issues are coming back to haunt them. You can almost hear the cries, "Oh, no, there it is again!" When probably the biggest truth of what's happening is the negative states are already clearing from your field. Your job at this point is to take a deep breath, relax and happily wave "Bye-bye!" to these old conditions.

Here are common negative discordant energies students have seen in their Grounding connection:

- The colors brown, gray, frozen white or black
- Trauma, abuse pictures and memories
- Holes in your psychic space

Grounding ... Coming Home To Your *Self*

- Metal plates blocking the flow of healing energies
- Boulders blocking the healthy energies of the body
- The Grounding Cord feels like or resembles backed-up plumbing
- Depression gray
- Feelings of nausea
- Feeling cold
- Headache
- Inability to focus or think clearly

If you see anything resembling these conditions, relax, take a deep breath, don't force but simply allow your body to Ground, affirm that you want to give these unhealthy emotional states to the Earth where they'll be effortlessly managed for you.

Don't worry—you are not polluting the Earth with your emotional garbage. Rather, think of the Earth as a large recycling plant that transmutes negative emotional states back to the perfected pattern of healthy loving energy. Actually, the force of nature is the strongest power that permeates all things. The power of nature or Creation is the same thing as the power of love. So as you Ground and give to the Earth your discordance, she transforms them back to the original essence of love. And that's

Chapter 5: Refining Grounding

what we call a healing and that's a beautiful thing...

Grounding Affirmations

- Build a relationship with the Earth, and begin to have a conversation with the consciousness of the Earth and simply say, "Hello, Earth!" Make your Earth relationship a personal one. You may be delightfully surprised with the good feelings you experience through your connection and rapport with the energies of the Earth.

- Write an affirmation in your own words conveying the idea that you want to feel more pleasurable Earth energies flowing throughout your body at all times. It can include thoughts or feelings that you always have everything you'll ever need for your life. The following are some examples:

I am Grounded and centered in my personal space.

I am fully present and Grounded in Now time.

I feel healing Earth energies pulsing through my body all the time.

Grounding... Coming Home To Your *Self*

I am a friend to the Earth.

I maintain a constant Earth connection all the time.

The Earth constantly pulses through me, heals me and teaches me everywhere I go.

From my Grounded center, I now draw to me everything I need for this life to be as full, positive and as meaningful and purposeful as it can be.

Chapter 6
The Golden Flame Meditation

To further deepen your cord and your Grounding experience, there is a cleansing healing energy, called the Golden Flame that is accessed with a visualization technique. This is a symbol of a golden flame that you envision burning away all discordant energy in your Grounding Cord and in your body. You can also affirm that this cleansing flame enhances only pure love, light and the best aspects of your self and the biggest truth of who you are.

The Golden Flame is obviously working with the element of fire. Fire is an expression of a healing, cleansing power. In fact, you can simply work with the visualization of fire with the intention to burn all that you don't need. It's very efficient to incinerate abuse, fear issues or any negative issue that created a disassociation from being Grounded. This Golden Flame will clear discordance of all kinds and produce healing effects in your body.

The Golden Flame Cleansing Meditation

- Breathe and bring your awareness within the center of your being.
- Envision the core of the Earth as a big reservoir of Golden Flame lava floating deep down inside the Earth, which is about what the inner Earth looks like anyway.
- Begin to see the Golden Flame coming up throughout the Grounding Cord and cleansing anything that doesn't belong there.
- Continue to bring Golden Flame throughout your body, especially if you experience a blockage, stress, pain, anger, tightness or discomfort of any kind. Affirm blazing the Golden Flame through that kind of substance energy until the feeling dissipates.
- Golden Flame is a very easy energy to access and visualize allowing it to course through you. Do this for a minute or two or as long as is comfortable.

Chapter 6: The Golden Flame Meditation

- As you complete working with the Golden Flame, put your focus on your Grounding into the Earth again.
- Throughout the day, it's good to work with an affirmation, "I now activate the Golden Fire to cleanse every sub-atomic particle of my being!" will also activate the cleansing of this powerful healing energy. It's not uncommon to notice that it's a lot easier to Ground with grace and ease after working with this powerful, cleansing Golden Flame energy.
- If you make this part of your daily practice, you'll be able to Ground deeper and your feelings of personal power will increase.

Here's what students working with this energy had to say:

I've cleared my Grounding Cord and body before, but nothing comparable to the cleansing power of the Golden Flame. I felt like it was clearing very quickly and sort of incinerating everything that wasn't supporting my life. All the perfected patterns within me were enhanced, while incinerating much of what was distorted.

Grounding . . . Coming Home To Your *Self*

Oh, it just feels really amazing. I feel like the cord really expanded after doing the Golden Flame and then I felt so solidly connected to the Earth. It's very, very strong. And I saw gold and orange rays of light coming up the Grounding Cord into me. And I felt little pings in different parts of my body during the meditation. I started going through my different health issues, to try to work on those and that felt really great. Because, at first, there were some places where the flame couldn't quite go through. But, now, there's a real flow to my Grounding Cord. So, I feel that if I started to do this every day, I could really address those blockages that I still have and work through them.

It's very calming...from being in a fire in the center of the Earth and coming up and sort of resonating with so much light...It's sedating in a way. It's enlivening but also has a nurturing quality, which I experience as very relaxing and peaceful.

I love the idea of the Golden Flame energies in my heart. It made me quite emotional. Then it just feels incredible. I've learned something new that I can do with my Grounding.

Chapter 6: The Golden Flame Meditation

Even the energy patterns of physical issues, can often times be helped with the use of the Golden Flame, as well as spiritual issues, mental issues, emotional issues, the whole spectrum. With each Golden Flame Meditation, incinerating the blocks, abuse, distortions and negativity will ultimately allow your Grounding to become deeper. Always take a moment to notice this after each clearing.

Healing the Grounding Cord...

To perform a healing of the Grounding Cord is easy and makes your Grounding more efficient. No one wants a weak, twisted Grounding Cord, with holes in it, or blockages resembling backed-up plumbing with lots of scary pictures around it. Right? So if your Grounding Cord resembles any of the above mentioned or simply isn't working properly or just doesn't feel quite right, you may simply need to heal the Grounding Cord by clearing negativity and performing a healing so that your healthy, functional Grounding Cord begins to emerge. Your perfected Grounding Cord should be strong, clear, open, fluid, comfortable, flowing and straight down into the core of the Earth.

Use the Golden Flame to heal your Grounding Cord to a state of perfection. Incinerate anything that could block the flow of Earth energy infusing through your Grounding Cord and throughout your body. This is an excellent way to learn to direct the healing energy of the Golden Flame to a particular part of your energy anatomy.

The Golden Flame Meditation for Healing the Grounding Cord

- Relax and breathe.
- Visualize the Earth's core as a vast reservoir of Golden Flame energy.
- Extend your personal Grounding Cord and make a connection from your body into the Golden Flame energies of the Earth.
- Begin directing the Golden Flame up through your Grounding Cord.
- If there's a place where your Grounding connection feels unsure, or has black spots, holes, the places where it's deviated, try to make your Grounding Cord straight as much as you can. If you don't see your Grounding but simply know it doesn't feel

Chapter 6: The Golden Flame Meditation

quite right, then continue with the healing for better results.
- Bring Golden Flame Healing Earth Energy into the places with the intention that this will repair the Grounding Cord, and make it functional and activate all perfected patterns.
- If you're unable to bring your Grounding down into the Earth's core, envision bringing the core of the Earth up to you. Simply affirm bringing that big pool of Golden Flame light in the Earth's core to the base of your spine. This is healing energy that can do anything you intend it to do with the focus of your mind.
- With the power of your mind, intention and will, you can heal many conditions. So bring the Golden Flame energy into anything that is in need of repair, such as old trauma or abuse issues.
- When you've cleared as much as you comfortably can, re-ground into the Earth and flush your body once more with the Golden Flame energies until every place inside your body feels replenished.
- You may need to do this again, or a few times until the energy shifts. But over time, your work will pay off with a nice strong, functional Grounding

Cord that will serve as a nice foundation for your life that helps you to manifest your goals and actualize your dreams.

Below, a student shares her Golden Flame healing experience:

The first time I tried Grounding I had tremendous obstacles between my Grounding Cord and the Earth's core. I kept trying different approaches and nothing worked. Finally, I began clearing my Grounding Cord and energy field with the Golden Flame and, when I went to ground again, it was easier and more effortless and deeper than ever before. Very smooth, very nice!

Other Uses for the Golden Flame

You can use this Golden Flame Meditation with the intention of clearing of bad habits that you'd like to be rid of, such as eating sweets, drinking alcohol or whatever it might be. It's always a good idea to release addiction as it interferes with your growth and acts as a type of distraction from your purpose in life. All

Chapter 6: The Golden Flame Meditation

forms of addiction are about looking for the fundamental spiritual connection to Source in all the wrong places. Addictions may give you a temporary sense of that connection for a short while and then you have to eat another piece of sugar in order to feel sweetness in life again.

Whatever that comfort food or substance is, you're looking for something outside yourself to make you feel good. But most of these habits are only a momentary feeling, whereas Earth energy establishes your energies at all times which nurtures, supports and heals. This is a great way to feel a fundamental support in a healthier and more sustaining way.

Essentially, everyone is looking for love. Ultimately, this is what everybody wants. So, here you are, consciously Grounding—the goal of which is to reach that place inside yourself which is more creative and loving. The opposite of that would be staying stuck constantly doing the same old unhealthy patterns over and over again, wishing, hoping for a different result or temporarily distracting yourself from your pain.

Grounding ... Coming Home To Your *Self*

The Golden Flame is a very efficient healing energy. It heals, it clears, it repairs, it re-patterns. It does it all. It'll help you to manage several issues at one time. This is a wonderful healing tool that will realign inside yourself and will assist you in getting anchored even stronger than ever. Continue to Ground and to work with the Golden Flame for a more profound experience of being in your body.

Your best teacher in the whole wide world is you actually doing these techniques. This is where you'll learn the most—not by reading about it or talking about it. Grounding is not an intellectual process. This is very much about actually doing and practicing with the intention that you're taking care of yourself. In so doing, you'll begin to access moments of brilliance and recognize when you're in the right place. It'll feel like you've come home to your Self and found the place and connection within you that you've been searching for all along.

Chapter 7
Grounding and Healing

If you think you came into this life with a set of problems and issues that you're powerless to do anything about, think again. Energy healing is a system that empowers you to alter circumstances in your life. By directing a healing energy with the intention and focus of your mind to the places in your body that are uncomfortable or stressed, you can alleviate distortions, and enjoy more freedom from the past to welcome more creative pursuits into your life.

Whenever your negative issues surface, begin to change your thinking about this state. Think about embracing your healing process and being responsible to consciously manage these issues in a mature, practi-

Grounding ... Coming Home To Your *Self*

cal manner. Your Grounding helps you to clear these types of dysfunction from your daily experience and is a beautiful way to perform self-healing for freedom from these unwanted influences. Know that simply by Grounding, a person begins to clear negativity from their bodies as it drains into the Earth and gets instantly neutralized. Now there may be a mountain of issues or even mountain ranges of issues keeping you from Grounding, but do not be discouraged and just keep doing the process daily or even Ground several times a day for better results. With these simple techniques, you can do so much of your personal clearings on your own.

When a person Grounds into the Earth, the healing energies are present within the Earth ready to be helpful and healing to you. With your mind and your creative visualizations working in concert with your will, thought and intention, you can alleviate discordance from your field and access healing energies to assist you. You have all the healing tools you need inside yourself.

Chapter 7: Grounding and Healing

You already know that creative visualizations help you to perform clearings and healings on yourself. Certain elements carry their own particular healing vibratory quality, which is quite beneficial. You've already worked with the element of Earth Gold and the Golden Flame energies. Now, expand your repertoire of healing energies to work with other elements as the power of various gemstones, such as ruby, sapphire, pearl and turquoise.

Grounding with Ruby

Ruby is a reddish, precious gemstone. Some rubies range from pink to deep reds and are usually quite beautiful. The energetic vibration of Ruby has a strong concentration of life-force energy and can be visualized and used for healing. This healing energy is very supportive and helps you to achieve success in life. Ruby feels very nurturing, wonderful and healing. It defines your boundaries so you can feel extraordinarily clear. It also supports you in manifesting your goals. The following is a good example of how Ruby energy helped me in a particular life situation.

Ruby Grounding and Dealing with People with an Attitude

Once I worked as a private duty nurse for a 91-year old millionairess in Marin county named Grace. Grace and I engaged in our daily games of Gin Rummy and Dominoes. After all, she'd played these types of games all her life and was quite good at it. She was practically rabid about winning which I didn't mind so much if it gave her such pleasure in life. If I won that was fine, but Grace usually won 80-90% of all the games.

What I did have issue with was Grace's ridiculous superiority attitude after she'd won. She particularly liked to come within an inch of my face to gloat and belittle me as her opponent in the most demeaning ways. At first, I quietly endured her snide remarks, her intrusiveness and competitiveness more from a place of mild surprise that she needed to make such a big deal of winning. Besides, I couldn't see confronting a 91 year-old acting like a jerk over card games. But day after day of this type of treatment was getting to be just a bit much for this private duty nurse.

Chapter 7: Grounding and Healing

One day I thought, "Surely there must be something I can do to put a stop to this, in my own special way." My intuitive voice instantly said, "Ground into Ruby." Grounding into Ruby meant doing a visualization technique of extending my Grounding Cord into the core of the Earth symbolized as a huge mother-lode of the gem stone Ruby. Some days it resembled a big piece of raw Ruby and other days it appeared as a magnificently cut, jewelry-store quality Ruby. Other days, the Ruby energy seemed like a large pool of liquid Ruby energy, feeling exquisite and unconditionally supportive of me. I trusted the process and worked with each of them as they appeared with the most excellent results.

As I Grounded into the Ruby energies of the Earth, much to my surprise I became an overnight success at card games. In fact, I was unbeatable. "Gin!" I announced after my first winning. At first her reaction continued to be demeaning, "You! Let me see those cards!" she said in a commanding voice. "Hmm, must be beginner's luck!" she said. But over and over, I ended many Gin Rummy games with the same word. "Gin!" "Gin!" "Gin!" each time spreading my hand of cards on the table and watching Grace have jaw-dropping moments of disbelief.

This did get Grace's attention and she began to look at me quite differently, more as a person commanding respect rather than a doormat for her to wipe her feet on. She became friendlier and more vulnerable and shared more about her life as we became really good friends. As time went on, our card games took a very different tone. Grace never, ever belittled me again.

Ruby Grounding Meditation

The following meditation is a way to work with the healing frequency of the gemstone, Ruby:

- Take a deep breath and close your eyes.
- Relax. Bring your awareness to the base of your spine.
- Envision a large pool of Liquid Ruby in the center of the Earth.
- Extend your Grounding cord into the Earth and be aware of connecting into the Liquid Ruby energy.

Chapter 7: Grounding and Healing

- Feel this sensation. Attune your body's energy to the Ruby energies.
- Notice if the Liquid Ruby changes your body, your emotions or your perceptions.
- With your intention, begin to draw Liquid Ruby into your body.
- Bring this energy to the level of your heart and from there broadcast Ruby energy throughout your entire body with extra emphasis or attention to any problem areas.
- When you feel saturated, envision the excess Liquid Ruby spouting out of the top of your head like a fountain filling up your aura to the front, sides and back of your body. (Pay special attention to the back.)
- Imagine that the Liquid Ruby is filling the area under your feet and above your head.
- When your body feels saturated with Ruby, re-ground into the Earth. Does your body feel different? Are you calmer and feeling more comfortable inside your own skin?
- Breathe deeply and affirm that will maintain this Grounded connection and wear Ruby energy in your aura for the rest of the day.

Other Elements for Grounding and Healing

You can use the above meditation but substitute any of the following elements for your healing energy:

Sapphire is a very dark blue gemstone. Some Sapphires are so dark blue they're almost black. The energy of Sapphire feels very refined and is wonderful to work with as it very efficiently absorbs the vibration of pain. This should be happy news to those sensitive types who feel the pain of the world or if many of your issues include processing pain. Working with Liquid Sapphire absorbs pain in a very gentle way. This is also a good energy to use for pain issues in children, or when you need to be very, very gentle. Sapphire is also great for protection. Filling your aura with Liquid Sapphire is a marvelous cloaking device, which ensures your need for privacy and protection from unwanted influences.

Pearl is a beautiful energy that nurtures the body and allows for integration of spirit and the physical body.

Chapter 7: Grounding and Healing

One student said it best with her description of her meditation experience:

My symbol and color for my Grounding is this lovely, giant pool of liquid pearl. This energy helps me integrate my physical body and my spirit with the power of the feminine added in. I love it! It's very beautiful and feels fantastic! The function of the liquid Pearl is to educate my whole body and to fill all the spaces so I can truly feel confident and express my true self. I know that I've consciously filled my body with the best parts of myself coming together plus an empowered sense of female spirituality, power, intuition, healing and artistry. My body feels great!

Turquoise is an energy that helps you to lighten-up and get back to a playful, child-like innocence. It helps to bring laughter and enjoying the levity of life. This is another important healing energy for humor and fun.

Once a client was coming to see me for a session and I could tell he was angry. I also saw that he was projecting his anger at me. I noticed that he was going to

Grounding . . . Coming Home To Your *Self*

ring my doorbell in about 10 minutes. I immediately began to Ground at Turquoise and filled my aura with this gorgeous blue turquoise. By the time I opened the door to greet him, all he had to do was look at me and instantly, he seemed to forget about his anger. Remember, enlightenment means lighten-up!

Chapter 8
Grounding and Self-Responsibility

As has already been established, when you begin to Ground more consciously and proactively, issues that kept you from being Grounded may begin to surface. Now you may be someone who will avoid Grounding at all costs after reading that sentence. Or you may be the type of person who sees opportunities for your personal growth from Grounding. As soon as you make the commitment to be more present in a responsible way, you instantly begin to draw from your inner strength and courage to be more fully engaged with all your faculties to manifest the life of your own choosing with clarity and direction. If this is your intention, the forces inside you instantly gather, enliven and recombine to make this so.

Grounding . . . Coming Home To Your *Self*

Grounding is a tremendous opportunity to manage the energies that keep you from being happy, successful, and actualizing your goals. It is for this reason that I've shared with you several meditation and healing exercises to use your personal Grounding as a basis for clearing and healing the subtle aspects of your energy anatomy. These Grounding and healing techniques help you to manage the obstacles and re-direct the course of your life on your own terms.

It's truly sobering to realize that no one is going to save you from anything. Exactly at what point do you begin to change the course of your life that's not working for you? And if you change your life and others begin to change their lives by being more responsibly Grounded, what effect could this have on the whole planet?

As you make a better connection to your Self and to the Earth, you change your consciousness that hopefully makes the world a better place of connected, dynamic, courageous individuals who work through their issues by choosing to become empowered, clear and strong. If we become a world of responsible, conscious, empowered

Chapter 8: Grounding and Self-Responsibility

people, would this not alter the course of our future at an individual level as well as at a national level or even at a global level? Is it not worth a try?

Various spiritual disciplines and philosophies teach that the world you see around you is a reflection of what's inside you. If this is true, then we'd better get busy, as it would appear there is much work to do. On the following pages are some suggestions that you can do on a daily basis:

Stop the war inside yourself!

I've heard people say they don't like war, but then they shrug their shoulders and say, "But there's nothing I can do about that." If what you see in the world is a reflection of what's inside, then perhaps there's more battle energy within you than you think. By taking responsibility to deal with your internal war issues in all its expressions, all forms of destructiveness, animosity, hatred, revenge, control, overpowering others, fault-finding, malicious gossip, feelings of jealousy and negativity, could this actually decrease the war vibration from this Earth? Every day of your life, you make

Grounding... Coming Home To Your *Self*

choices about engaging in war-like behavior in your interaction with others.

Dissention between people can create a type of war energy in your personal life, which contributes to the negativity on this planet. Making healthier more empowering choices while not contributing to these negative emotional states, taking responsibility and healing these issues within your Self clears that energy from you and from the Earth. Ground into the Earth and dedicate being Grounded to reclaim your power and demand to live in a world that makes sense and that represents the interests, intelligence and consciousness of all people.

Stop all blame of others for your position in life. Whenever you begin the conversation of blaming others, you're wasting valuable time when you could get on with your life and take charge of your personal situation. Instead of disgracing another, work on your Grounding to help you arrive at the place in life where you want to be. Approach this as a commitment to yourself that you are willing to make. Since success in life requires that you be devoted to your Self and your

Chapter 8: Grounding and Self-Responsibility

own path, use your creative energies toward building your own life on your own terms. Make better choices for yourself and you'll build a path to your personal success and make better use of your time and your beautiful creative energies.

Stop comparing yourself to others... Do you ever wonder why others are successful instead of you? Do you become jealous, resentful or angry of people who take risks and secretly wish to see them fail? Oftentimes successful people make their life's work look effortless, and others wrongly assume that they've not earned that status in life. This very well could be misplaced anger at your self for missing opportunities! Get on with your own life, do your own work on yourself for this will certainly get you where you want to go rather than trying to make yourself feel uplifted by putting others down. Jealously, back-biting, competitiveness and divisiveness hardly ever further your goals. Hard work, clear perception and insight, decisive action, taking risks, will.

Stop the Pity Party... feeling sorry for one's self accomplishes absolutely nothing. This type of fascination is nothing more than a distraction from your own process and personal self-discovery. This disassociation from your own source of personal power and growth could have been caused by any number of issues that require healing. Once again, get on with your personal work and learn Grounding and a healing process and take your personal power back.

Resentment towards others for past hurts will certainly keep you stuck in places in life where you really don't want to be. Resentment will never heal the pain and anger you feel but will only beget more negativity in your life. Sometimes it's simply more important to be free than it is to be right.

Grounding into Liquid Silver Forgiveness

Grounding into Liquid Silver Forgiveness is one of the most important healing energies to bring final closure to issues so we can move forward during these times of fast-paced transformation. The healing vibration of forgiveness is invaluable in healing, repairing and re-patterning the widest variety of conditions that other-

Chapter 8: Grounding and Self-Responsibility

wise keep one stuck and fixated in unpleasant states and conditions. Forgiveness energy brings comfort and completion to issues, it helps a person be remarkably neutral so that one stays centered and clear. If there's a healing energy that will help you live through these challenging times of change, while bringing resolution to the past, it's this one.

All you need to do to access this energy is envision a fluid silver energy and affirm that this represents the vibration of forgiveness. Does it matter who you're forgiving or anything like that? No, not particularly. But you may have a particular person in mind whom you need to forgive, which is also understandable. But mainly, you can use Liquid Silver Forgiveness as a generic healing energy irrespective of the issues.

Sometimes, we simply need to move on and say goodbye to the past—no matter what the storyline or the particulars are about. What an empowering realization when one understands that true freedom comes from making this decision and getting on with your personal healing. Liquid Silver Forgiveness is one of the very best energies to work with as it heals the broadest

Grounding . . . Coming Home To Your *Self*

variety of issues, mending and erasing old wounds, and erasing abuse energies from your body. When in doubt, ground into Liquid Silver Forgiveness and let this course throughout your body. Forgiveness educates you to be conscious of seeing the big picture reality and discerning what is really important and what is the greatest truth about an issue.

Liquid Silver Forgiveness Grounding Meditation

Sit in a comfortable place. Use the Chi Gong Exercise for Stress with hands resting lightly on your lap.
- Take a deep breath and come to a relaxing feeling of comfort in your own body.
- Listen to the sound of your own breath—inhaling and exhaling.
- Bring your awareness to the base of your spine.
- Within the deep central core of the Earth, visualize a vast pool of Liquid Silver.
- Extend your Grounding Cord into the Earth's core with the intention of connecting into the large pool of Liquid Silver affirming that this represents the vibration of forgiveness.

Chapter 8: Grounding and Self-Responsibility

- Ground into the center of the pool of Liquid Silver Forgiveness and simply feel this connection, and rest here for a moment attuning to these energies and simply feeling them.
- When the moment feels right, visualize that your Grounding Cord is stirring the Liquid Silver Forgiveness. Get a sense of the consistency of this energy and make a visceral connection to this frequency.
- Imagine that through your Grounding Cord you begin to draw the Liquid Silver Forgiveness into your body, filling every space to top capacity from your toes to the top of your head. Immerse yourself in Liquid Silver Forgiveness and open your senses to the quality of this energy.
- Affirm that the Liquid Silver Forgiveness energy flows through you and throughout your physical body, emotional body, mental body and spiritual body.
- You have approximately 25,000 genetic codes located in every cell of your body. Affirm saturating Liquid Silver Forgiveness through every one of your genes bringing forgiveness throughout everything in the genetic material of your body. Spend a few moments doing this.

Grounding... Coming Home To Your *Self*

- If there's a place of tension or pain in your body, affirm that you are directing this flow of energy to that part of your body and allow it to permeate through that space for as long as is comfortable.
- Notice the places within you where this energy has been. Your body should feel more relaxed, open, free and clear.
- Take a deep breath and feel the freedom from issues of your past allowing you to move forward in life with a greater sense of freedom.

If you do this everyday, you'll notice the results bit by bit. Anyone can perform this type of healing. It's easy, it's simple and it works. What a good feeling it is to clear unwanted issues cluttering your energy field and your body. Bringing finality to these negative states can lead to personal freedom and more life-affirming creative pursuits. Very cool!

Chapter 9
Grounding and Creation

After a few years of Grounding, I began to ponder about what is it that makes this simple Grounding technique so powerful? What is really creating all these benefits? I began to think about the Earth and how powerful she is and that the biggest force inside of me and within the Earth and everything is a force of nature—it's the power of Creation. If Grounding brings everything to a focal point, does this not bring us into an alignment where we begin to access the biggest force in the universe—the power of Creation? I began to think so.

These thoughts led me to meditate on this force of nature more consciously in my personal meditations and as I hiked through nature. On my walks, I would attune to the Creation force inside me and then feel it all around me. I began feeling really beautiful within myself and I could sense this force in all the leaves, trees, in the soil in everything. Not all hikes were filled with this sense, though I consciously worked with these energies. But when I did feel this sense, it was sublime and there was nothing like it. From these experiences, I created the following meditation:

Grounding and Creation Meditation

Indigenous people worship the sun as the greatest source of Creation. They honor the sustenance given them by the greatest light source there is—the sun! The core of the Earth is filled with molten lava, which resembles the sun in the sky. Use this visualization to help you picture a sun deep within the core of the Earth. Obviously, this is a big energy that's quite powerful. Stretch your consciousness to attune your body with this force of nature to awaken feelings of freedom, expansion and power within yourself. This visualization and following exercise will help you see yourself as a piece of Creation and to build healthier references to Earth and nature that's more intelligent, powerful and conscious.

Chapter 9: Grounding and Creation

- Take a deep breath and relax.
- Attune to the power of the Earth.
- Get a sense of Earth energy as bright as the sun in the sky—a bright light source deep within the Earth.
- Allow the force of gravity to take your Grounding Cord into the Earth's core and begin to feel the quality of this energy. Once you feel you've accessed this place, notice how this energy looks, feels and any impressions you receive about this magnificent Earth energy.
- Envision your Grounding Cord as a giant honey spoon, stirring the Earth energy and getting a visceral sense to further establish a substantial Grounding connection.
- From this Grounded place, begin to attune to the force of Creation or nature that is in all things—it's in the Earth, it's within you, it's in everything. Attune to this force until you're aware of its presence in all things and hold this setting for as long as is comfortable. The force of Creation is the most powerful and fundamental energy there is. Build a more profound relationship and awareness with the power of Creation in nature, in you and in all things.

- A daily practice of this meditation will strengthen your ability to see the power of Creation everywhere, which is a great constructive, positive energy from which to build your life. With this energy your thinking will change to begin to see in your life potential, creativity, ideas, the interconnectedness of all things, a whole new paradigm of perception. The longer you allow this force to broadcast throughout your entire body, you begin to re-educate your body for health and to help you remember the greatness of your being.

Grounding with the California Redwoods

Living in the San Francisco Bay Area opened my world to the beautiful hiking trails of Marin County, the expansive Pacific Ocean and the Golden Gate Recreational Area, to nature, to the Redwoods, and to one of my long time friends, Mt. Tamalpais. Hiking has always been an important part of my life, as I love the outdoors and feeling the magical energies in that area has always been so spiritually nurturing and wonderful.

Chapter 9: Grounding and Creation

On many walks through nature, I loved to stand with my back against the massive redwoods and feel the bold power of the trees. The California Redwoods beautifully symbolize being dynamically present as well as large, bold and powerful. I decided that they were to be my teachers. I used to attune to them for how to be really Grounded, how to be powerful and to be big and expanded and to take up more space in the world. Rather than feeling small and disconnected from nature, I wanted to be the giants that they were, so spiritually empowering, strong and present. The force of the Creation energies is very apparent with the California Redwood giants and to commune with them and learn from them is a profound teaching. The power of nature is the perfect teacher. By observing the forces of nature, you become so much more aware about how to live your life in harmony with the Earth, all creatures and all living things.

Your relation to Creation is important to reclaim feeling and being alive. If you ever feel stuck or lost and you don't know what to do in your life, simply attune to the force of nature and place your attention on your Grounding Cord. You'll begin to access the answers

Grounding . . . Coming Home To *Self*

you were seeking, connect with people you need to connect as synchronicity begins to flow.

Being in Nature is extremely helpful to Grounding. Activities such as camping and hiking in nature provide a big burst of life force energy that's very nourishing, and it's easier to anchor into the Earth because you are sleeping on the earth and walking on the Earth. The Creation energy is easier to attune to in the forests much more so than in the cities and it's easier to make the connection and it feels like coming home to your self which is a really good healing. People in large cities like to visit the parks and go camping to dispel their busy lives into the Earth. The Earth becomes the all-time recycling plant as it takes in the busy chaos from your body and instantly transmutes that energy into Creation.

Creation Energy is synonymous with the LOVE vibration ~ which is the biggest truth about who we really are. Our lives are all about getting back to this basic fundamental premise of expressing our loving nature and making that more pronounced in our lives. More than ever we need to be a solid Grounding force and

Chapter 9: Grounding and Creation

this is what Creation provides—a constructive, life-affirming, positive energy in our personal lives and in this world. The more you take a stand for the life-affirming source of all Creation in your life, it takes your focus off the destructive elements so that you truly begin to create and build your life in alignment with the force of Creation and to create all aspects of your life in the power of love.

Grounding with Creation in Mt. Shasta

The area of Mt. Shasta, CA is an exquisite jewel of nature providing so much inspiration and sheer beauty. Amid the gorgeous waterfalls, breathtaking vistas from the mountain, meadows of colorful field flowers, I've often walked the trails and attuned to the life-force teeming all around me. This was yet another glorious opportunity to be aware of the Creation force in the leaves, in the streams, the water, the wildflowers, it was teeming all around. As I walked, I turned my awareness to this force within me while consciously aligning to these forces outside of me. After a while of this focus and awareness, I began to feel quite expansive and loving inside myself as the link between my

Grounding ... Coming Home To Your *Self*

inner and outer self grew stronger and stronger the more I felt this. To attune to Creation energy like this is absolutely sublime as there's a feeling of a calm peace, sweetness and a memory of connection that I used to have but somehow lost. To restore your fundamental connection to these magnificent forces helps you remember that you are a part of all of this.

These types of "Walking Meditations" are enlivening and feel wonderful. This is the state that makes life feel sublime and very much worth living. While some people chase material things to fill the void in their lives, nothing seemed more precious than this very fundamental awareness and connectedness. From this state, answers to life's problems simply presented themselves. Simply attuning to this state and being there felt amazing as I felt as comfortable and at home within myself as I've ever felt. How could something so simple be so profoundly important? The longer I stayed in this state, the more centered, neutral and empowered I felt. This is a place that everyone can find simply by attuning to it as this force is in everything and you can find these energies anywhere. It's that simple.

Chapter 9: Grounding and Creation

- Begin to attune to the life affirming force of Creation all around you until your body is resonating with this marvelous energy.
- Ground into the Earth and affirm holding this energy setting for the next 24 hrs. Do this process everyday for a few minutes per day or as often as you'd like.

These are simple yet powerful processes that will assist you to be more present and to build your ability to be a more integrated and whole human being. Here's one student's experience:

As I began to Ground, I've become really inspired. It's been really great for me. I'm having many creative ideas come to mind and it almost feels like my true path is unfolding as to what I really want to be doing in my life. It continues to unfold and grow and I feel that alignment when I Ground into the Earth. I just feel really strong and inspired. This is so great!"

Grounding . . . Coming Home To Your *Self*

Chapter 10
Frequently Asked Questions

Do I have to Ground every day?
For a while, yes, you do. Ground every day for as much or as little as you want. Ground several times throughout the day, wherever you are, no matter what you are doing. Make it a part of your everyday practice. The more attention you give it, you make your Grounding stronger and stronger. After a while of this daily practice, you'll be Grounded all the time. But at first you may need to become conscious and aware to build a strong foundation for your life.

Do I have to do all these healing meditations you've suggested everyday?
No, of course not. Pick and choose the one or ones that feel right for you and only do that one or a couple. After

Grounding ... Coming Home To Your *Self*

a while, you'll feel complete with that particular process. Then you can find another to work with until you've completed your personal process with that one. This way you'll become intimately more connected to each of healing energies suggested in this book, and then you'll begin to find some of your own symbols to work with, just like I did.

My physical body feels really dense when I Ground and I actually question if this is a good setting for me. Am I in the right place?
When a person has lived most of their life out of their body and then they begin to get more Grounded, they may feel a physical sensation that is heavy and dense. I can assure you; the added density is not a bad thing. It's a very positive state to establish a reference point for how to live your life from this place at all times. One student had this to say about the feeling of density: As soon as I went to that Grounding place, my whole body just sank deeper and I realized that I was Grounded and I got it! I imagine sitting on a field of grass and absorbing Earth energy as my connection sinks deeper. And...I do feel heavier.

Chapter 10: Frequently Asked Questions

I love the powerful imagery of the Earth Sun to help me with Grounding, but sometimes I begin to feel overwhelmed by the power of that. Any suggestions?
It's good to anchor into the Earth Sun and feel the power of it. If it's overwhelming, work with simple images like sitting on the grass or some other visual that feels good and reassuring to you. To whatever degree you can feel comfortable befriending the nurturing healing energies of the Earth and allowing this sensation to be felt throughout your whole system is the goal. And whatever creative visualization helps you to achieve your goal is wonderful.

I've been doing all this healing work on myself, I thought I'd feel better, but in some ways I feel worse.
Please, do not be discouraged as this will eventually dissipate. If you continue with the process, you will clear the negativity from your field and you will feel a lot more free and easy. Depending on how much clearing is needed, you may initially hear yourself saying, "Is this ever going to end?" But it will, and every aspect of your life will work much better. Remember, if you can't do the work yourself, get some help to lose the psychic weight and come home to your Grounded beautiful true Self...

Grounding ... Coming Home To Your *Self*

I cleared some issues from my field and then I could feel some of them coming back. What's that about? Another very important point is to Ground after a clearing and to completely fill your body with Earth energies. If you clear the density and negativity and leave your field empty, the human body doesn't deal well with emptiness. In truth, it would rather have the old issues in there rather than nothing at all. Or if you don't take the time to saturate your space, with Earth energy after a clearing, there can be a variation of the old issues coming back into your field. So when you Ground, and after you've done a clearing, always remember to affirm or visualize directing the Earth energies into every cell of your body. Fill to full capacity! Be very generous with this part, as there's a lot of Earth energies to be generous with. Always remember to make a point of filling up your body with some kind of light, color or energy. Think about what you would rather have, as if to say to yourself, "OK, the old issues are gone now. I'm at a point where I have a choice about what I'd rather have. I want to replace the old issues with love, light, wholeness, stability and happiness. I want to completely fill my body with new information of what it means to be truly connected and inte-

Chapter 10: Frequently Asked Questions

grated as a whole human being on every level of my existence." Make bold intentions!

I am having difficulty feeling the Grounding process. I'm not sure to what degree I really feel the Earth energy. Any suggestions?
When it's difficult to feel your own Grounding or the Earth energy, this is an indicator that there's usually some density in the lower part of the body that blocks your ability to feel. Instead of mentally pushing through that, your efforts would best be served by actually doing a clearing of the issues in your emotional and feeling bodies. What is it that needs to be cleared? It could be myriads of things—usually it's a backlog of unresolved emotional issues you forgot you had, trauma & abuse from the past, parts of you that have become numb usually to not feel the pain or other feelings of discomfort or to protect yourself. When these are cleared, your body will feel lighter, happier, your thinking clearer, and you get a taste of your own essence energies, rather than a persona you've adapted your life to in order to survive. In other words the feeling body begins to function as it was originally designed and you begin to feel again.

Grounding . . . Coming Home To Your *Self*

I would suggest that you work with any of the clearing or healing meditations listed in this book. And then begin to Ground deeper and get a deeper sense and feeling of the Earth energy. Once you clear the density, than you'll have a better experience of being in and actually feeling your body. Clarify your personal psychic space and your sense of self gets expanded and more defined.

How can I be Grounded without mentally "forcing." Since energy follows my thought, shouldn't I try to push through mentally?
I understand your wanting to push mentally for Grounding to occur, but try working with the Golden Flame energies instead and then learn to Ground in a more effortless way. Grounding should be easy and never forced. By the way, when I say "Energy follows thought," what I actually mean is, "If Grounding is your intention, all the energies of your body come together to create a more Grounded experience for you." So mentally pushing doesn't do anything except perhaps some mental strain, frustration and possibly a headache. Intention is hugely important in this work. For best results, be focused, precise and always clear in your intentions.

Chapter 10: Frequently Asked Questions

Sometimes I find myself trying to push that Grounding with will and a mental drive to make it happen. Then I realized that this was not proper Grounding. It is more allowing myself to flow with the force of gravity that naturally deepens my Earth connection—yes?

You are correct. If you find yourself working too hard at Grounding, you're not doing it properly. This is a process that you cannot use will power or too much pushy analytical thinking power to muscle your way to Grounding. Rather, it is a full-body visceral process that you learn to use your whole body, mind, emotions and spirit to Ground into the Earth.

I sometimes fill the void of my life by overeating and lethargy instead of Grounding. Why do these habits seem so appealing instead of healthier lifestyle changes and choices?

You are so right about feeling ungrounded and trying to fill that void with an unhealthy habit, such as overeating. This is quite common. Overeating does make a person "feel" more Grounded. But unfortunately, this is only a temporary fix as usually within 30 minutes, people need to eat again to regain that nice Grounded feeling. Clearing the underlying issues

Grounding... Coming Home To Your *Self*

for your unhappiness and establishing a good Earth connection will restore a lasting balance, stability and feelings of well-being in your life.

Grounding simply takes practice. The more you do it, the better and more anchored it becomes. If you simply do the Grounding and the Golden Flame clearing, or any of the Grounding Meditations in this book, it will get better. If it becomes too difficult, do get some help!

I've been doing Grounding work and I'm feeling really blocked. What's that about?
Some people feel wonderful being Grounded, but that's not always the way it goes. Initially, Grounding has been known to stir up some negative issues that you'd long ago forgotten about. Many structures that are responsible for your unhappiness surface and it's suddenly difficult to ignore them anymore and the last thing you want to do is be Grounded, so the mind creates a block that seems insurmountable. This is an incredible opportunity for you to take responsibility for these types of blocks and issues. Because whether you're conscious of it or not, that blockage issue is affecting your ability to be fully present, happy, peace-

Chapter 10: Frequently Asked Questions

ful and functional. Make a commitment that you'll do some healing on yourself everyday and chip away at the energy blocks and suffering that's deep within and allow your wonderful self to shine through.

While clearing my Grounding Cord, it disintegrated like dust and blew away. Why would it do that?

If ever you have an experience of your Grounding cord disintegrating into dust or disappearing, or any number of bizarre experiences, this generally represents aspects of yourself that do not want to cooperate with the process, or parts of yourself unwilling to be fully Grounded. Usually this is some sort of fundamental built-in fear—or even survival energy that feels too vulnerable to be present. No worries, when the body will not cooperate with this process, there's a clever way to approach this. But, first, you need to be very respectful of what your body can comfortably do and not push it. Usually there's no small reason why your body is unwilling to be fully here. I would suggest that you work with Gratitude energy for a gentle, reassuring clearing. Ground into a large pool of gratitude and visualize a grateful energy filling up all aspects of yourself. Infuse gratitude to all fear and resistance

Grounding . . . Coming Home To Your *Self*

for the years of service of keeping you safe and protected by reminding you that you ought not be so powerful and capable lest you be harmed. Realize that the blocks are a part of yourself doing what they can to keep you feeling secure. When in truth, they're aspects of you unconsciously working against yourself, without you realizing it. Instead of being hard on yourself for not cooperating, be extremely gentle and respectful. This part of yourself needs to be acknowledged that it's done a brilliant job of keeping you safe for a long, long time. It also needs to be notified that the job you gave it to do is complete and it needs an upgrade or a promotion to keep you safe and protected in a new and efficient way. So fill with gratitude, give all these old outdated protective structures to the Earth and give your self a new job to now keep you Grounded and protected in a more efficient present-time sense.

I've been Grounding and meditating and I feel like this is going so slowly. What do I do?
The reason why you feel you've been Grounding and doing all that meditation but it's going slowly for you—this is a form of fear, resistance or trepidation

Chapter 10: Frequently Asked Questions

energy. Often times, fear and mental energy combine to create a fixated pattern in the psyche that refuses to do anything other than hold that frozen-fear state. It may be that you need to manage the fear energy in your body. Ground into a large pool of gratitude and then bring that energy throughout your body and fill yourself up to the brim with gratitude. When the body is so filled with gratitude you begin filling up the aura with that energy. I suggest you work with this image and specifically target any fear energies in your body that are afraid to move forward. This will help all areas of your life clear away old personas that no longer serve and begin your life anew in the present without the trappings of the past.

Do you have to be Grounded to work with the Golden Flame energy because I don't think I'm quite there.
You do not have to be Grounded to visualize the Golden Flame. This is another excellent tool that helps all situations where Grounding is difficult. You can do an affirmation, if it's too difficult to visualize. Just the affirmation, "I am a being of Golden Fire," or "I am Golden Fire" over and over again for approxi-

mately 15 minutes 3 times daily for an excellent way to facilitate a great change.

I feel there are many negative associations within the Earth. Why would I want to be Grounded here?
Some times people don't want to be Grounded due to old belief systems which keep them from feeling safe here. These types of negative thought associations with the Earth energy are just another energy to clear from your space so you can begin to make peace with simply being here. A really good energy to work with for issues such as this one is Liquid Silver Forgiveness energy, so that you can clear these associations and become comfortable here on Earth. Like it or not, you are here and whatever you can do to try to become more comfortable, loving, and feeling pleasurable being in our bodies on the Earth is a good aspiration to strive for while you're here.

Sometimes I find I have an easier time with Grounding using my breath. Is this useful?
Certainly! The breath is very powerful and quite useful for getting out of your way and allowing these ener-

Chapter 10: Frequently Asked Questions

gies to flow through you. Here's a simple technique called "Grounding on the Breath:"

While inhaling, consciously breathe the Earth energy up through your Grounding Cord and affirm evenly distributing the healing Earth energies throughout your body. And when you exhale, consciously Ground down into the Earth making the fundamental connection while letting go of all that does not serve. Repeat this process over and over again. This creates a feeling of emanation of healing energies throughout your entire body and aura, which feels wonderful. Earth energy heals, clears, repairs, re-patterns. It very efficiently manages many issues all at one time. Some issues that may continue to interfere with this are old resistance, old fear, old energy that over time became locked at a particular setting. If you keep breathing and working through it, it'll eventually give way. One person had this experience:

At first, I had a really hard time concentrating, my mind was distracted, and then I remembered to use the conscious Breathe while Grounding and all of sudden I felt a really big sense of calmness.

Grounding ... Coming Home To Your *Self*

One of the things I've noticed in visualizing a Grounding Cord going down, as soon as I do that, I have a good feelings tickling up & down my spine. What does this mean?

This is a symptom that more energy is flowing up & down the spine. It's flowing through the body, which is a good thing. Sometimes it will feel like carbonated bubbles through your body, or feelings of pulsing, tingling, and wonderful states of lightness and relaxation.

How can Grounding help me release the stress from my body?

You'll notice that when your energies are chaotic, disassociated and fragmented, Grounding helps to pull you together in a more cohesive, integrated way. So whenever you begin to feel the integration within yourself, everything calms inside you and the stress factor is immediately reduced. The Grounding Cord acts as a garbage chute, all the stress in your body is constantly flowing out of your body and Grounding into the Earth where it gets instantly neutralized. How sweet is that?

Chapter 10: Frequently Asked Questions

Once I learn the Grounding process, are there things I can do to make the Grounding Cord even deeper and more powerful?
Once you understand how important Grounding is and you become more proficient with it, there are things you can do to stretch the perimeters of your Grounding and learn some variations to make it stronger and even better. You can stretch and deepen the Grounding Cord and widen it to expand those settings and get more empowered and experience more presence of mind. Practice Grounding as you've never before. This will help to reeducate your body and to fill the spaces in your body and psyche where there are voids and emptiness. Consciously filling up the space with the power and the intelligence of Earth energy is a beautiful thing. This facilitates the integration of spirit and matter in an empowering way.

Sometimes it's hard for me to extend my Grounding Cord into the Earth so deeply. Is it OK to bring the Earth Sun up to my Grounding?
Yes, what a great idea! Bringing the core of the Earth to you rather than going to the core is a clever adapta-

Grounding ... Coming Home To Your *Self*

tion to work with some of the difficulties and challenges that come your way when you begin to Ground.

I'm not used to feeling spiritual while being deeply rooted to the Earth. Somehow this feels strange. Can you please explain that?

It's quite common for spiritual people to feel light, airy, out-of-body and ethereal. People associate this with spiritual feelings and it feels right to them. If they've somehow identified being spiritual as being out of body, then to be profoundly Grounded seems odd somehow. How then do we begin to find a pleasurable sensation and identify being spiritual while maintaining a connection to the Earth? Indigenous people have had a connection to nature and Creation as a base for their spiritual practices for thousands of years. It's time to awaken as indigenous people do—consciously and spiritually while honoring our physical relationship to all that is.

Made in United States
North Haven, CT
07 June 2024